THE SUN

by L. L. Owens

The Child's World

Published by The Child's World®
1980 Lookout Drive • Mankato, MN 56003-1705
800-599-READ • www.childsworld.com

ACKNOWLEDGMENTS
The Child's World®: Mary Berendes, Publishing Director
The Design Lab: Design and production
Red Line Editorial: Editorial direction

PHOTO CREDITS
NASA/courtesy of nasaimages.org, cover, 1, 3, 4, 6, 9, 10, 12, 16, 26, 27, 29, 31, 32; Shutterstock Images, 5, 19; NASA/courtesy of nasaimages. org/The Design Lab, 6, 7, 13; Zhou kun qd/AP Images, 11; Andrejs Pidjass/ Shutterstock Images, 15; Kokhanchikov/Shutterstock Images, 17; NASA GSFC/courtesy of nasaimages.org, 21; NASA/Goddard Space Flight Center Scientific Visualization Studio/courtesy of nasaimages.org, 23; The Exploratorium/NASA/courtesy of nasaimages.org, 25

LIBRARY OF CONGRESS CATALOGING-IN-PUBLICATION DATA
Owens, L. L.
 The sun / by L.L. Owens.
    p. cm.
 Includes bibliographical references and index.
 ISBN 978-1-60954-388-4 (library bound : alk. paper)
 1. Sun—Juvenile literature. I. Title.
 QB521.5.O94 2010
 523.7—dc22
                          2010040461

Printed in the United States of America
Mankato, MN
December, 2010
PA02072

ON THE COVER
In this image, the hottest parts of the sun appear almost white and cooler areas appear red.

Table of Contents

The Sun and the Solar System

How do you know it's daytime? The sun is shining! Even on a cloudy day, the sun makes daylight. The sun is the brightest star in the sky.

The sun is Earth's most important space neighbor. It is at the center of the **solar system**. The planets go around, or **orbit**, the sun.

From Earth, we see beautiful sunrises and sunsets because of Earth's rotation.

5

SUN

Fun Facts

NUMBER OF PLANETS
ORBITING: Eight

DISTANCE FROM EARTH: 93 million
miles (150 million km)

SIZE: The distance around the sun's middle
is about 2.7 million miles (4.3 million km).
That is about 108 times bigger than Earth's
middle!

AVERAGE SURFACE TEMPERATURE: 10,000°F
(5,500°C)

OUR SOLAR SYSTEM: Our solar system has eight
planets and five **dwarf planets**. Pluto used to be called a
planet. But in 2006, scientists decided to call it a dwarf planet
instead. Scientists hope to discover even more dwarf planets in
our solar system!

Mercury

Venus

Earth

Mars

Ceres

Jupiter

Our Solar System

Saturn

Uranus

Neptune

Pluto

Haumea

Makemake

Eris

Planet

Dwarf Planet

What Is a Star?

A star is a spinning ball of burning **gas**. The gas creates light and heat. That's what we see—and feel—on Earth. Scientists don't know how many stars there are in the universe. But there could be billions of trillions of stars!

You could not stand on the sun, even if it weren't burning. Unlike Earth, the sun has no solid surface. It is made of layers of gas.

The sun is a medium-sized star. Other stars in the universe are much larger.

Our solar system is a small part of the vast universe. The sun is the only star in our solar system. Stars twinkling in our night sky are billions of miles away. The sun is *millions* of miles away. It's close enough to light up our world!

Astronomers study stars in the night sky.

11

A Closer Look

On Earth each day, the sun rises in the east and sets in the west. At noon, the sun is overhead.

Is the sun changing its position? No way! The sun only appears to move as Earth spins, or rotates, on its **axis**. One full turn of Earth equals one day—the time from one sunrise to the next sunrise. Even though the sun doesn't change position, it spins on its axis, too.

Fun Fact

Long ago, ancient Greeks did not know the sun was a star. They believed the sun god Apollo rode a chariot of fire across the sky. That is how he lit the world from sunrise to sunset!

An axis runs through the center of the sun. The sun spins on the axis.

Life and the Sun

Has your skin ever been sunburned after a sunny day at the beach? Does standing in the warm summer sun make you feel good? The sun affects the weather, your mood, and even your health.

Humans need the sun for many reasons.

The sun is one reason there is life on Earth. The sun's **gravity** keeps Earth and other planets orbiting around it. This strong pull keeps Earth from floating off into space.

The sun also warms the planet. It helps keep wind and water moving and affects our weather.

Fun Fact

Earth would be completely frozen without heat from the sun.

The warm sun melts the snow in the spring.

17

The sun is the source of all food on Earth. It makes our green plants grow. Humans eat plants. Or, we eat animals that eat those plants. We couldn't live without the sun.

The sun gives us energy in other ways. Sunlight can be used as **fuel** to power calculators, homes, and even cars. Unlike other fuels, sunlight doesn't cause pollution.

Solar panels can be installed on the roofs of homes to make sunlight into electricity.

Exploring the Sun

How do scientists explore the sun? Remember, they can't visit. It is far too hot—and there's no place to land!

From Earth, scientists use special cameras and **telescopes** to observe the sun. They also send spacecraft to collect **data** closer to the sun.

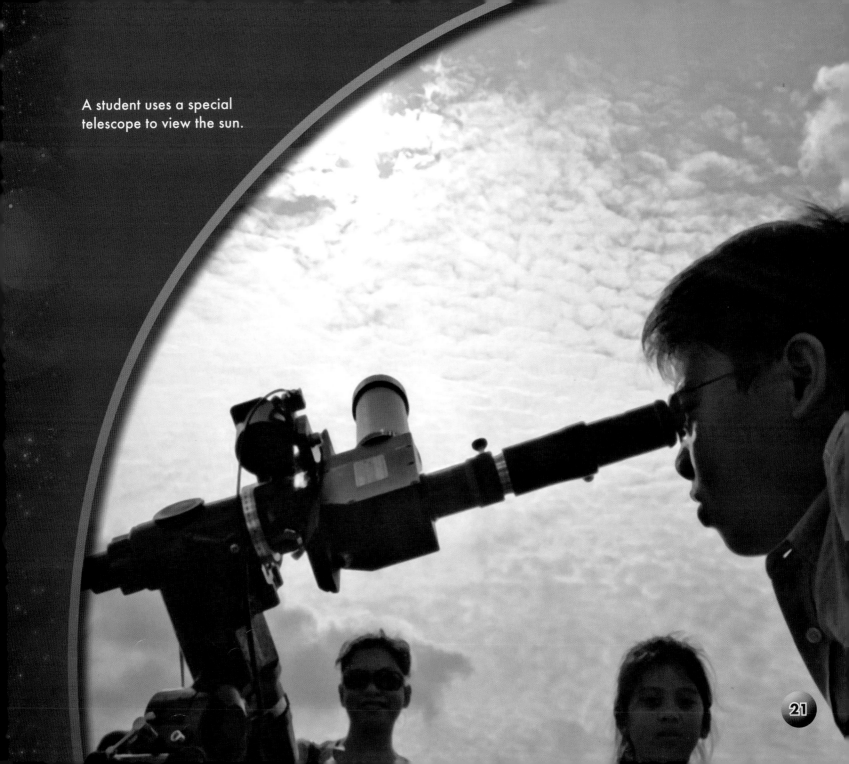

A student uses a special
telescope to view the sun.

Using strong telescopes, scientists can safely see the sun's surface. They see dark blotches called sunspots.

Sunspots are cooler areas on the sun. But they are still scorching hot. Sunspot temperatures average 7,000°F (3,900°C). That's more than 50 times hotter than Earth's hottest temperature.

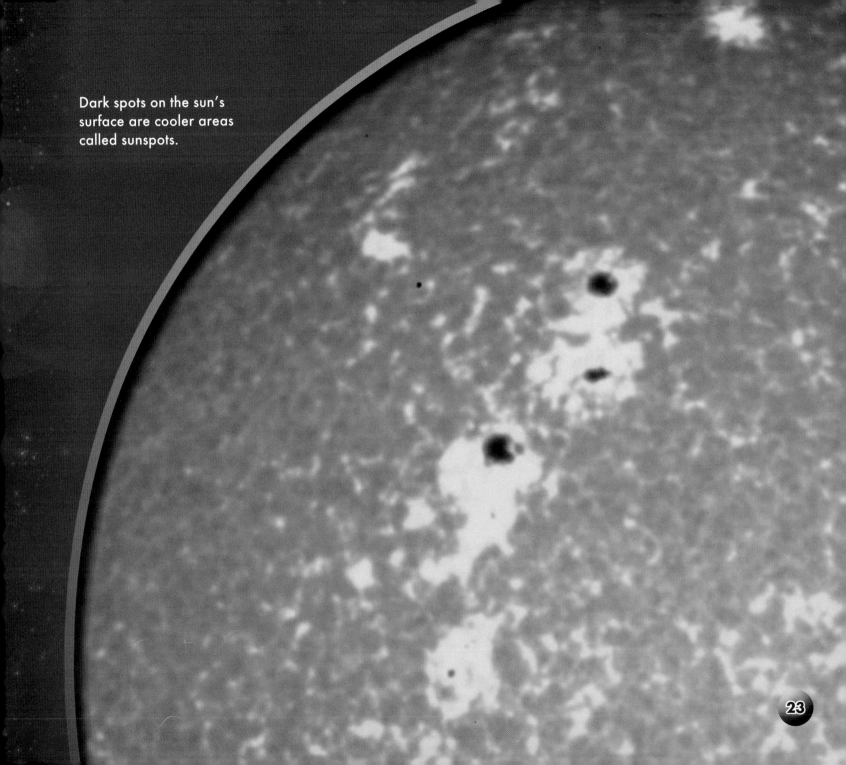

Dark spots on the sun's surface are cooler areas called sunspots.

Deep in the center of the sun is its core. It is the hottest part of the sun. It reaches 27 million degrees F (15 million degrees C). The bright **photosphere** is the layer of gas that gives us the sunlight we see. It is the lowest layer of the sun's **atmosphere**. This layer is so hot it shines.

The corona is the outermost layer of the sun's atmosphere. The corona is visible when the moon passes in front of the sun.

NASA has been studying the sun for many years. In 1995, NASA launched the *SOHO* spacecraft. It studies the sun's many layers.

Fun Fact

NASA stands for the National Aeronautics and Space Administration. It is a US agency that studies space and the planets.

The *SOHO* spacecraft launched aboard a rocket in 1995.

Scientists now know that the sun is always changing. *SOHO* can predict powerful sun blasts. These can cause electrical power outages right here on Earth.

It is important to keep learning about the sun. Scientists are looking for new ways to use free energy from the sun. New discoveries will help us predict the future of life on Earth—and how we can make it better.

An artist created this image of the *SOHO* spacecraft in space.

GLOSSARY

astronomers (uh-STRON-uh-merz): Astronomers are people who study planets, stars, or moons. Astronomers often use telescopes to study stars in the night sky.

atmosphere (AT-muhss-fihr): An atmosphere is the mixture of gases around a planet or a star. The photosphere is one layer of the sun's atmosphere.

axis (AK-siss): An axis is an imaginary line that runs through the center of a planet or a moon. Earth rotates on its axis.

data (DAY-tuh): Data are facts, figures, and other information. Scientists hope to gather more data about the sun.

dwarf planets (DWORF PLAN-itz): Dwarf planets are round bodies in space that orbit the sun, are not moons, and are not large enough to clear away their paths around the sun. Dwarf planets often have similar objects that orbit near them.

fuel (FYOO-uhl): Fuel is a substance that is used for heat or power. Sunlight can be used as fuel.

gas (GASS): A gas is a substance that moves around freely and can spread out. The sun is a ball of burning gas.

gravity (GRAV-uh-tee): Gravity is a force that pulls objects toward each other. Gravity pulls Earth along its path in orbit around the sun.

light-year (LITE-yihr): A light-year is a measure of the distance that light can travel in one year. Scientists use light-years to measure great distances in outer space.

orbit (OR-bit): To orbit is to travel around another body in space, often in an oval path. Planets in our solar system orbit the sun.

photosphere (FOH-tuh-sfihr): The photosphere is the lowest layer of the sun's atmosphere. The sun's photosphere is so hot it shines.

solar system (SOH-lur SISS-tum): Our solar system is made up of the sun, eight planets and their moons, and smaller bodies that orbit the sun. The sun is the center of our solar system.

telescopes (TEL-uh-skohps): Telescopes are tools for making faraway objects appear closer. Scientists learn about the sun using telescopes.

FURTHER INFORMATION

BOOKS

Jefferis, David. *The Sun: Our Local Star*. New York: Crabtree Publishing Company, 2008.

Landau, Elaine. *The Sun*. New York: Children's Press, 2008.

Trammel, Howard K. *The Solar System*. New York: Children's Press, 2010.

WEB SITES

Visit our Web site for links about the sun: **childsworld.com/links**

Note to Parents, Teachers, and Librarians: We routinely verify our Web links to make sure they are safe and active sites. So encourage your readers to check them out!

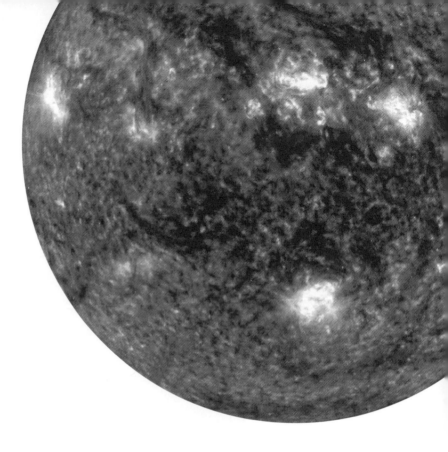

INDEX

ABOUT THE AUTHOR
L. L. Owens has been writing books for
children since 1998. She writes both fiction
and nonfiction and especially loves helping
kids explore the world around them.